The Desert Rats

The Desert Rats were units of the British 8th Army who fought in North Africa from 1940 to 1943. But the war they fought was unlike any the world has ever known. Instead of manpower, mobility was the important thing, the ability to move fast through the treacherous desert terrain. Gigantic campaigns of movement, massive milling conflicts between fleets of tanks and armoured cars surged in the hot choking sand.

In this fascinating book, the author tells how badly Britain needed to defeat the German panzer divisions, led by the brilliant Rommel, the "Desert Fox." He evokes what life was like for the troops, and describes how day after day the tanks would grind forward, then mass together, their caterpillar tracks screeching across the flinty ground, ready for the great battles – from the dramatic defence of Tobruk, to the great clash at Alamein, and finally to the desperate struggle in Tunisia and the rout of the Nazi enemy from the shores of North Africa.

A WAYLAND SENTINEL BOOK

The Desert Rats

Matthew Holden

"On with the task, and good hunting to you all!"
Viscount Montgomery, speaking to 8th Army troops
(12th November, 1942).

WAYLAND PUBLISHERS LONDON

More Sentinel Books

The Story of Gunpowder   *Kenneth Allen*
The Legions of Rome   *Matthew Holden*
Tourney and Joust   *Steven Jeffreys*
Nelson's Navy   *Roger Hart*
War in the Trenches   *Matthew Holden*
A Medieval Siege   *Steven Jeffreys*
Genghis Khan and the Mongols   *Michael Gibson*
The Battle of Britain   *Anthony Hobbs*
The Wars of the Roses   *Kenneth Allen*
The Crusades   *Matthew Holden*
The Samurai of Japan   *Michael Gibson*
Battle of the Atlantic   *Kenneth Allen*
The French Foreign Legion   *Nigel Thomas*
Cavaliers and Roundheads   *Michael Gibson*
The Story of the Navy   *Anthony Hobbs*

frontispiece: A Desert Rat relaxes with a cup of tea and a letter from home before starting out on patrol (1942).

SBN 85340 217 5
Copyright © 1973 by Wayland (Publishers) Ltd
101 Grays Inn Road London WC1
Set in 'Monophoto' Baskerville and
printed offset litho in Great Britain by
Page Bros (Norwich) Ltd, Norwich

Contents

List of Illustrations

1. The Desert Rats

Winston Churchill lights another fat cigar before rising slowly to his feet. Before him sit rows of officers and men; the sun beats down upon the North African desert around them, and, nearby, tanks and armoured cars shimmer in the heat.

"In days to come," says Churchill to the soldiers, "when people ask you what you did in the Second World War, it will be enough to say: 'I marched with the 8th Army.'"

Many of the tanks standing waiting on the sand have a badge painted on their armour. The emblem shows a small distinctive animal, with a long curled tail and strong back legs, something like a tiny kangaroo. The animal's proper name is the jerboa, and it lives in the wastelands of North Africa. It can survive in almost impossible conditions, and bounds with gigantic leaps from one scrap of cover to the next.

The jerboa has another name. And the animal and its nickname have been chosen as mascot by one of the most famous groups of soldiers in the whole of the Second World War – the Desert Rats. These men live in the wilderness with their tanks and armoured cars, and move in leaps and bounds – like the jerboas.

But who are the Desert Rats? In the early months of fighting against the Germans and Italians, they made up a small body of men of the British 7th Armoured Division. Later the name became so famous and so respected that it spread to cover the

entire British army to which the 7th Armoured Division belonged – the 8th Army. The regiments and divisions of the 8th Army were in turn pitted against an equally famous enemy: the German *Afrika Korps*, led by Erwin Rommel, "The Desert Fox."

Above The British Prime Minister, Winston Churchill, hoists his topee on a stick to wave farewell to 8th Army troops during his tour of the western desert (August, 1942).

Victory at Tunis

Streets and houses seem deserted as British tanks rumble down the road from the hills. Open doors flap miserably in the hot wind; windows gape wide; pavements are empty; rubble spreads onto the road from shattered homes, and walls are pock-marked by bullets and shell splinters.

The time is early afternoon, 7th May, 1943. British troops are just outside Tunis, their last objective in North Africa. The Germans are retreating, hoping to be snatched from the North African shores before this last sea escape route can be severed. Tunis, the final refuge, has been abandoned.

British units advance cautiously into the city. Within minutes those deserted streets are crammed with joyful Tunisians, who have slipped from hiding to welcome the liberating forces. Women weep; men toss up bottles of wine to the dusty troops on the vehicles; girls festoon the tanks and armoured cars with garlands of flowers.

Only a few days remain before the completion of the gigantic North African campaign – Egypt, Libya, Tripolitania and Tunisia are now clear of the Italian and German army. The road to Tunis has been long and painful, signposted by many great battles – El Agheila, Gazala, Sidi Rezegh, Mersa Matruh, Alam Halfa, Alamein. The Germans have proved a stubborn foe, and British successes have been matched by enemy counter-offensives; ground won has been lost, and won again.

Now, at last, the troops can taste victory. And among those armoured cars standing in the centre of Tunis are some which have the jerboa painted on their sides. They belong to the 11th Hussars, perhaps the most famous of all the Desert Rat regiments.

These men were present at the very start of the campaign three years before. And now they are here for the kill.

Perhaps, as they stand by their armoured vehicles, they remember the struggles which lie behind, the friends lost, the hardships endured, the battles fought, the wounds suffered – all the events and experiences which make up the story of the brave Desert Rats.

Opposite and below The rapturous reception given to British and American forces as they enter Tunis (May, 1943). The capture of Tunis meant the end of German hopes in North Africa.

Desert Commanders

The men of the 11th Hussars represented only one very small section of a massive force. The 8th Army to which they belonged was made up of hundreds of similar units – squadrons, battalions, regiments, brigades, divisions and corps. At the time of the battle of Alamein in October, 1942, this mighty gathering totalled about 150,000 men.

All these men had to be organized, controlled and directed in battle. Responsibility for this fell upon two men, one in Cairo and the other with the army itself. At the time of Alamein these two officers were General Bernard Montgomery, commander of the 8th Army, and his superior, General Harold Alexander, Commander-in-Chief of Middle East Command.

British leaders changed during the long North African campaign. Montgomery is perhaps the most famous – colourful, yet strict, a man who disliked smoking, drinking or late hours, yet who liked to wear unconventional uniform. "Monty" became a hero, and crowds flocked around him whenever he went home to England.

Alexander, on the other hand, remained in the background at his headquarters in Cairo. He was quiet, modest, handsome and courteous. He provided Montgomery with all he needed up at the front, and his efficiency proved superb.

Other leaders also found fame in the desert and in Cairo. The first Middle East Commander was General Sir Archibald Wavell, another quiet and modest man, who loved poetry and literature – yet who could also display courage and military daring. He was replaced by General Sir Claude Auchinleck, tall and dominating, known popularly as "The

Opposite General Bernard
Montgomery, better known as
"Monty," perhaps the most
famous and best loved of all
British commanders in the
Middle East.
Below General Alexander, on
the left, walks through the
mud with two colleagues at
the 8th Army headquarters,
Lieutenant-General Allenby
and General Alanbrooke
(January, 1944).

Auk." He in turn gave way to Alexander.

"Good generals," wrote Wavell, "will never reach the first rank without much study of their profession; but they must have certain natural gifts – the power of quick decision, judgement, boldness, and, I am afraid, a considerable degree of toughness, almost callousness."

The men in charge of the 8th Army possessed all these natural gifts, and the Desert Rats relied on them for their survival. They had to live daily under terrible strain, caused by the weather, the harsh country, their responsibilities – and by the courage and determination of the enemy.

The enemy

British troops had a strong respect for their enemy, and especially for the much-vaunted German *Afrika Korps*. On 11th January, 1941, the German Nazi leader Adolf Hitler declared that German troops should be sent to North Africa to help out the Italians. Until then the Italians had faced the British on their own – and had suffered humiliation and defeat.

Opposite A group of German and Italian prisoners captured in Libya (May, 1942). British soldiers often commented on the difference in attitude between enemy prisoners – the Italians were usually cheerful and laughing, while the Germans seemed subdued, as if disappointed at not having achieved what they set out to do.

Now German troops began to pour across the Mediterranean into Italy's territories in North Africa – Tripolitania and Libya. Yet no great liking existed between the *Afrika Korps* and the Italian armies, even though they fought on the same side. Most Germans believed their "friends" to be lazy and weak, overfond of wine, good food and comfort.

The Germans on the other hand were dedicated and determined. They thrived on discipline. Their organization was superb, and their equipment extremely efficient. This difference was even reflected among the enemy prisoners taken by the British. One Desert Rat officer described the arrival of captured German soldiers: "There are about 150 of them . . . most of them wearing dusty grey jackets and trousers, brown boots and long-peaked 'engine-driver' caps. They behave quietly and seem preoccupied . . . "

He added: "Another column of prisoners comes in, this time all Italians. They too look dishevelled and dusty, but are in quite good spirits. Most appear to have brought their blankets with them, and with their ill-fitting bluish coats, voluminously sagging plus-four breeches and many extraneous bundles of personal belongings, look for all the world like a troop of touring cyclists, bereft of bicycles . . . One of the Italians has a small white dog, which frisks about with friend and foe alike."

The German training was tough, aimed at providing maximum speed, flexibility and confidence. At the peak of German successes in North Africa, all these qualities were developed by their most famous leader, Rommel, the notorious Desert Fox.

The Desert Fox

Above Field Marshal Erwin Rommel, commander of the German *Afrika Korps* (1941–43). Because of his daring cunning, and his great skill in this new form of mobile warfare, Rommel soon became known as "the Desert Fox."

British politicians, assembled in the House of Commons on 27th January, 1942, were astonished to hear the Prime Minister give praise to an enemy commander, and moreover one who had recently inflicted on British forces in North Africa a severe defeat.

"We have a very daring and skilful opponent against us," declared Churchill, "and, may I say across the havoc of war, a great general." Some listeners grumbled at the Prime Minister for thus praising an enemy leader in time of war.

But this leader was unlike any other enemy commander. By virtue of his courage, skill and daring, Rommel was indeed a special case. British troops in North Africa spoke of him almost with awe, so much so that General Auchinleck felt obliged to issue a special order to his officers, which declared: "There exists a real danger that our friend Rommel is becoming a kind of magician or bogey-man to our troops, who are talking too much about him . . . I wish you to dispel by all possible means the idea that Rommel represents anything more than an ordinary German general . . ."

Yet Auchinleck knew, as clearly as did Churchill and the British troops, that Rommel was in fact no "ordinary German general." So too did the Germans who served under him. He had the ability to dominate the battlefield, even though he himself officially served under an Italian supremo named Bastico.

Rommel was keen-eyed, energetic and imaginative, and expected his troops to be as tough as he was himself. One of his officers wrote that he "was not an easy man to serve; he spared those around him as little as he spared himself. An iron constitution and nerves of steel were needed to work with Rommel."

Yet Rommel could also be kind and very human. "I'm very well," he wrote to his worried wife during the thick of the fighting. "I've just spent four days in a desert counter-attack with nothing to wash with . . . It's our twenty-fifth wedding anniversary today . . . I want to thank you for all your love and kindness through the years."

Left Hands in pockets, Rommel ponders in the Libyan desert while one of his aides studies the horizon through binoculars (1942). Rommel worked relentlessly, and expected those around him to do the same.

Chivalry in arms

Rommel believed in waging "war without hatred;" and the Desert Rats agreed. A strange kind of chivalry existed in the North African campaign. Troops would fight hard, and to the death; but they also respected their enemy.

General von Ravenstein, commander of a German division in the desert, wrote after the war: "If warriors of the Africa campaign meet today anywhere in the world, be they Englishmen or Scots, Germans or Italians, Indians, New Zealanders or

Below The harsh conditions of the desert imposed a new code of behaviour on those fighting there, and the different nationalities were bound together by certain informal rules. Here a group of "British" soldiers, including men from New Zealand, South Africa and Poland, gather round to examine a captured German wireless set.

South Africans, they greet each other as staunch old comrades. It is an invisible but strong link which binds them all. The fight in Africa was fierce, but fair. They respected each other and still do today."

Von Ravenstein's comment also revealed another feature of the North African campaign – the many different nationalities involved. His list was by no means complete: the "British" forces also included Poles, Nepalese Gurkhas, and Frenchmen. Language problems between the British and their allies were partly overcome by the use of a strange slang, a mixture of Arabic, Cockney and Indian words. One man might open a tin of meat and say to another: *"Taro china just shufty this. The kooloo's zift. Duff scoff peachy if Imbasha can't buddly 'em."* This meant: "Just a minute mate, just look at this. The whole lot's bad. It'll soon be a lousy meal if the corporal can't get them swopped."

Different nationalities were bound together by a code of behaviour which laid down certain informal rules. One Desert Rat officer told his men: "Your chief concern is not to endanger your comrade. Because of the risk that you may bring him, you do not light fires after sunset. You do not use his slit trench . . . Neither do you park your vehicle near the hole in the ground in which he lives. You do not borrow from him, and particularly you do not borrow those precious fluids, water and petrol . . . Of those things which you do, the first is to be hospitable and the second is to be courteous . . . A cup of tea, therefore, is proffered to all comers . . . This code is the sum of fellowship in the desert."

Above American soldiers in Tunisia spread a little cheer with this campfire built in an empty petrol can.

The battlefield

The Desert Rats shared a common experience with each other, and with the enemy – the desert. Popular ideas of the desert as endless golden sand-dunes are incorrect. Instead the countryside is covered with a variety of soils and rocks – gritty sand, fine sand, dark shingle, flint, hard-baked mud, limestone, gravel. The main vegetation is a stunted scrub called camelthorn, which survives off the dew from the Mediterranean Sea in the north.

The most important Desert Rat fighting took place around the 500-foot high Egyptian and Libyan plateau, which is bordered by the Mediterranean coastal strip in the north and the Sahara in in the south. The northern edge of the plateau drops steeply to the coastal area, and the few passes down this ridge were of vital military importance – the side which held places like Fuka, Halfaya and Sidi Rezegh could control the enemy's movements.

Few people inhabited this wild region before the vast armies arrived. Hundreds of miles separated the dirty, poverty-stricken villages; small groups of nomads roamed the wilderness. The desert had been left alone, except by the animals – jackals with their dismal howling, hyenas gibbering madly, and graceful gazelles. Insects abounded, as grotesque as their surroundings – huge camel-spiders, yellow and repulsive, black scorpions, and big pink tarantula spiders with the ominous "ace of spades" design on their bulbous backs.

Troops now had to live and fight in this unwelcoming land. They had to endure the terrible heat by day and the biting cold by night. They had to learn to live with a minimum of water – about a gallon a day for all their washing, cooking and drinking needs – when they craved for pint after pint to slake their fiery thirsts. They were burned

Below Map showing the main battle area in North Africa, 1940–42.

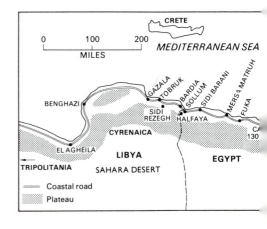

Above Polish troops stand guard in the rocky desert outside Tobruk (1941). Contrary to popular belief, the desert in North Africa is not all golden sand-dunes. In fact, the craggy barren landscape shown here is much more typical.

almost black by the sun, and wore only shorts, shirts, socks and boots.

In April, 1942, one soldier wrote home: "This must undoubtedly be the most unpleasant time of year in the desert, alternately hot and cold . . . When the wind's from the north, it blows chilly and desolate, but when it's from the south, out of the Sahara as today, it's far more disagreeable – dry, feverish and suffocating, making us twice as thirsty as usual . . ."

21

A new form of warfare

Below In the desert, war became extremely mobile, since tanks and armoured cars could motor almost anywhere. Here a lorry-load of British soldiers pause to have their photograph taken before joining the rest of their unit for manoeuvres in the desert. The gas masks are to stop the dust and sand from flying into their faces.

Desert conditions resulted in a new form of warfare. Apart from the coastal road in the north, there were few recognized routes, but on the plateau itself tanks and trucks could motor almost anywhere.

War became extremely mobile. Armies were no longer tied to roads and railways. Instead they plunged across the open countryside, moving fast and virtually free. This made desert fighting very similar to warfare at sea. The desert was like an ocean. The armoured cars acted as scouting destroy-

ers, while the guns and tanks became battleships and cruisers. Campaigns were fast flowing; armies covered vast distances. "On and on and on we went," wrote a Desert Rat, "the Brigade streaming out behind us like a huge armada of destroyers, each vehicle with its own little bow wave of dust and larger wake of churned-up sand."

As with naval warfare, territory proved to be largely unimportant. Victory did not go to the side which controlled the largest amount of land – the desert, like the sea, was worthless on its own. Victory went instead to the side which could sweep the enemy from the battleground and destroy its capacity to fight. No matter how much desert you could occupy, the enemy still remained a threat unless his army could be defeated. Indeed, the more desert you took, the greater your difficulties might become. All supplies, including precious petrol, had to be brought from the rear, or from key points such as Tobruk. And the longer the distance to the forward areas, the greater became the supply problems.

Time after time forces would push onwards, apparently victorious, only to be brought to a halt through shortage of supplies – their lines of communication had become too stretched. Or the enemy might turn in flight and suddenly strike back before their pursuers could consolidate. Desert warfare as a whole soon became a gigantic campaign of movement – sweeping attempts to move round the side of the enemy army to strike at his lines of communication, and massive milling conflicts took place between fleets of armoured vehicles.

Weapons of war

Panzer Mark IV
Weight: 20 tons
Speed: 25 m.p.h.
Crew: 5
Armament: 1x7mm. gun
2x7.9mm. machine guns

Left A German Mark IV
Panzer tank, the main battle
tank of the *Afrika Korps* for
almost its entire career. It was
extremely reliable, and was
ideally suited to the new form
of desert warfare.

In the desert war, everything depended on tanks,
and on the men who crewed them. Tremendous
efforts were made to develop better armoured
vehicles and to train their crews to greater efficiency.
"In a mobile action," wrote Rommel, "what counts
is material . . . The finest fighting man has no value
in mobile warfare without tanks, guns and vehicles.
A mobile force can be rendered unfit for action by
the destruction of its tanks, without having suffered
any casualties in manpower."

At the start of the war, British tanks were better
than those used by their Italian enemy. Then the
Germans arrived with still more efficient machines.
Moreover, Rommel trained his men so that the
tanks worked in close cooperation with anti-tank
guns – the tanks could attack while the anti-tank
weapons helped to punch a way through the enemy
defences, and to fend off Desert Rat counter-attacks.

The German *Panzer* tanks were soon found to be
better suited to the desert conditions than the

British equivalent – the Matilda, Valentine and U.S. Honey tanks. Later the British obtained massive Grant and Sherman tanks from America, with 77mm. guns; and gradually the advantage swung back to the Desert Rats. Yet the *Afrika Korps* had other points in their favour. First, their *Panzers* were developed from the same basic model, allowing easier interchange of parts and quicker repair time. Also the Germans had more suitable vehicles for re-covering broken-down tanks and bringing them back to be fixed up for battle again. Time and again the British were surprised by the number of tanks which the Germans could summon up in a fit state to fight when only a few days before they had suffered heavy casualties.

But the Desert Rats had America's vast factories on their side. The Atlantic convoys kept up a constant flow of armoured vehicles pouring into North Africa. So the Desert Rats grew steadily stronger, while the *Afrika Korps* slowly bled to death.

Above A soldier hurriedly shovels sand onto the wheels of his vehicle, which have caught fire after an enemy bombardment. Fire is the curse of the desert, and gives away valuable information to the enemy.

25

War without end

War seemed to stretch endlessly for the Desert Rats. On and on they moved, and the desert had no horizon.

Big battles played only a small part in this tremendous campaign; instead, most of the time, each side tried to wear the other down. Armies remained constantly on the move, or waiting to move. Each small unit had to be self-contained, ready to act on its own if necessary, ready to advance or retire at short notice. Each armoured car was its own storehouse, home and kitchen; each infantry section had a lorry carrying all the necessities of desert life.

One infantryman wrote: "Our section truck . . . is a 15-cwt Morris, entirely open fore and aft, battered and sand-stained, with divisional signs – a red jerboa in a white circle on a square red field – painted on the sides. She's called Mabel, after the driver's wife. All our gear and supplies have to go on board: each man's rifle and the section weapons including the Bren-gun . . . the Boyes anti-tank rifle, and several boxes of ammunition; a large Italian medical chest, picked up on a previous campaign, in which is kept our current supply of rations; another box containing the section reserve of tinned food . . .

"Then there are about half a dozen 2-gallon water-cans for daily use, and an equal number carried full as another 'untouchable' reserve; also four 4-gallon petrol-cans for general consumption, with a similar number containing the reserve; then the driver's tool-box, a spare-wheel, and several

spades. On top of this lot, everyone has to find room for his large pack, haversack, webbing equipment, overcoat and bedding-roll . . . " Each time the section halts, perhaps for only half a day, the whole load is taken out of the vehicle to ease the weight on the springs.

But soon the section has to move on again, in another wearying convoy. "The moon was up," wrote a Desert Rat in his diary. "The convoy moved in jerks. Three times we crashed into cars ahead or were crashed into by those behind. Almost impossible to see in the whirling, choking clouds of dust . . . "

Above Tanks of the British 9th Lancers pass along a road which has just been blown up by the enemy. Sappers are busy repairing it while the tanks thunder past in a choking cloud of dust.

27

"Up the Blue"

To be "Up the Blue," as the Desert Rats called the forward areas, was to lose all normal aspects of daily life – roads, trees, houses, shops, ordinary people. Small items usually taken for granted, minor comforts such as cigarettes or a cup of tea, took on a new importance.

"We get a buckshee [free] issue of fifty cigarettes a week," wrote an infantryman in his diary, "usually of rather poor quality . . . As long as there's no lack of char or fags everyone's happy." Another diary entry read: "Rations are very poor these days. For

Left Preparing the evening meal in the difficult conditions of the desert calls for great ingenuity. Here men of the 8th Army get busy mixing flour, water, milk, margarine, salt, and a few dried apple rings to make an apple pie.

breakfast, a slice of bread and bacon; for lunch, half a slice of bread and tinned pilchards; for dinner, meat stew and potatoes, rice and prunes."

And daily the men were harried by thousands of flies, attracted to the smell of their human sweat. "Soon after sunrise they arrive in hordes from nowhere, then plague us with malign persistence all through the day, swarming and buzzing around, trying desperately to land on our faces, in our eyes, ears and nostrils, on our arms, hands, knees and necks. And, once settled, they bite hard. Desert sores, oases of succulence, draw them like magnets . . ."

Men suffered from jaundice, heat exhaustion, dysentery, sunstroke, desert sores, rashes and blisters. Some even became ill from scurvy, like sailors did in the old days of sailing ships, and for the same reason – lack of fresh vegetables.

After a while even the most hardened Desert Rat would fall victim to "desert weariness." One soldier wrote: "For months now we've been cut off from nearly every aspect of civilized life, and every day has been cast in the same monotonous mould. The desert so saturates consciousness that it makes the mind as sterile as itself . . . Nothing in the landscape to rest or distract the eye; nothing to hear, but roaring truck engines; and nothing to smell but carbon exhaust fumes and the reek of petrol."

This dreary existence continued for day after scorching day. "We could never work out whether it was Monday, Wednesday or Friday or whatever it might be. The sun seemed to fry our brains. We didn't talk much about home, and when someone mentioned green fields or ice-cold pints of beer, they soon got shouted down. It hurt too much to hear of them."

Above A young soldier squats on an upturned oil can to write a letter home. The gauze wrapped round his head is mosquito netting, designed to keep the flies from getting in his mouth, his ears and his eyes.

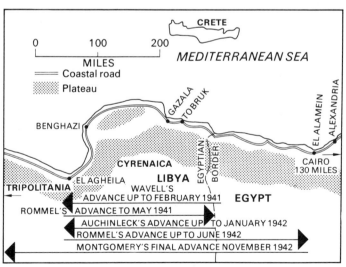

2. The birth of a legend

Most Desert Rats knew little about the tremendous events in North Africa in which they were taking part. They were only aware of the happenings immediately around them, in their section, company, battalion or perhaps division. Their main concern was their own survival, and that of their comrades. Knowledge of the campaign as a whole was reserved for only the most senior commanders; the rest remained in confusion and ignorance. Men were told to move to a certain point, to withdraw, to attack, to defend, and they did so without really knowing why. As one officer wrote in his diary: "It just is not possible to tell precisely what is happening. Distances are so great. Things move so quickly. Information is hard to come by."

Broadly speaking, however, the desert war was marked by a series of campaigns, which took the form of violent swings, backwards and forwards, as each side in turn won superiority. First the British advanced against the Italians in 1940 and early 1941; then the Germans under Rommel regained the ground they had lost, and advanced through most of 1941, before the Desert Rats started to push forward again at the end of the year – only to find themselves thrown back even further in 1942. Finally came the last campaign, starting at Alamein in October, 1942, after which the British advanced to ultimate victory. This is the bare outline of the exciting, heart-breaking, and finally triumphant story of the Desert Rats.

Top left Rommel directing his tanks and armoured cars as they advance into Egypt (Spring, 1942). The war in North Africa was marked by great sweeping campaigns, as each side tried to outflank the other.

Left Map of North Africa, showing the main campaign movements, 1941–42.

Britain's only hope

In 1940, when the North Africa story began, Britain's war position was desperate. In Europe, she stood alone against the military might of Germany who, since the outbreak of war in September, 1939, had overrun the whole continent in a series of lightning raids. France had fallen in June, 1940; British troops had barely been rescued from destruction at Dunkirk. The Battle of Britain was won in the summer of 1940 – "Spitfire Summer" – but only just, and many feared that this nerve-racking air struggle might soon be resumed.

The German bombing offensive against Britain, the Blitz, began in November, 1940. By the time it ended, nearly 43,000 people, men, women and children, had been killed. Russia remained a German ally. America had not yet entered the war to help Britain. Germany was superbly confident. Hitler had been forced to delay his threatened invasion of England, Operation Sealion, but many people in London expected the attack to be renewed as soon as the weather improved.

Britain's very survival seemed acutely threatened. Enemy submarines were taking a deadly toll in the grey wastes of the Atlantic – by August, 1940, $2\frac{1}{2}$ million tons of shipping had been sunk. Britain did not have sufficient warships to protect the convoys bringing in vital supplies, nor could the shipyards produce sufficient replacements for the ships sunk.

Britain had to face the possibility of slow starvation as German U-Boats continued to sever the Atlantic supply lines: food was increasingly rationed,

Above Adolf Hitler, the German Nazi dictator, addresses a crowded meeting of his supporters. His fiery rhetoric inflamed the German people, and led them to war.

Left A street scene in Balham, south-west London, in the autumn of 1940, as a bus disappears head-first down a bomb crater during one of the German raids on the city.

and war production of ammunition, weapons and tanks steadily declined. The country had no chance of resuming the offensive against Germany in Europe itself. Invasion of the Continent across the English Channel was quite out of the question while Germany remained so strong and Britain so weak.

Only in faraway North Africa could British units hope to attack with any chance of success. Upon the Desert Rats, therefore, rested all hopes of silencing the enemy's shouts of triumph.

First hostilities

Above An Italian gun crew take a rest in the sunshine (Libya, 1940). When the British attacked, they found the Italians ill-prepared, and had little difficulty in defeating them.

On 10th June, 1940, Germany received another ally – Italy declared war on Britain. And Italy had about 250,000 soldiers in her colonies of Cyrenaica (now part of Libya), and Tripolitania in North Africa, under the command of Marshal Graziani. Facing this army were General Wavell's 36,000 troops in British Egypt – who also had to be ready to strengthen the extremely weak garrisons in East Africa. To make matters worse, the British had far fewer tanks than the Italians.

Yet Wavell, the Commander-in-Chief, had ordered that, as soon as Italy declared war, an attack was to begin over the frontier of Egypt and into Libya. On the night of 11th June, within twenty-four hours of the official opening of hostilities, the peace of the desert was shattered as the 11th Hussars – part of the 7th Armoured Division – began their offensive.

These first attacks showed that the Italians were ill-prepared. But British successes could only be very limited while their resources remained so thin. The Italians pushed forward a little way. Then both sides waited – the British tried frantically to build up strength, while the Italians were gathering courage to attack.

The British struck first, in December, 1940. General O'Connor decided to use daring tactics to wipe out the Italians at the frontier of Egypt. The assault would be made by the 7th Royal Tank Regiment and a Brigade of the 4th Indian Division, who would sneak forward by night to a position behind the enemy line. The 7th Armoured Division would then punch forward; the enemy would be thrown into confusion and the Desert Force would sweep onward, hoping to reach Tobruk or even distant Benghazi.

British armoured units began to move shortly before dusk on 7th December. The tanks were almost hidden by clouds of dust, and only their turrets floated above the billowing sand clouds. Pennants fluttered; wireless aerials whipped to and fro; tank tracks screeched across the flinty ground. One driver wrote: "I feel calm now. The waiting has been worse. Now I have something to do. I feel numb, but I've stopped shaking. There seem to many of us that the Eyeties [Italians] won't have a chance."

Success at Sidi Barrani

Complete surprise was achieved. The British swept
westwards round the Italian positions at Sidi Barrani
to strike at their weakest point. Italian tanks were
shot to pieces before their engines could be warmed

Below After the tanks came the infantry units, their bayonets fixed for the charge, racing towards the enemy through the thick clouds of dust.

up. Black plumes of smoke soared skywards. And fifteen minutes behind the armoured vehicles came the infantry. Cameron Highlanders ran into the smoking Italian camp, bayonets fixed, while pipers paced slowly backwards and forwards, playing the charge. The wail of the bagpipes sounded eerily above the roar of the guns, the chatter of machine-guns, and the screams of the defenders.

Inside an hour, the attack was over. The Italians had been overwhelmed, with nearly 40,000 prisoners taken and 73 tanks and 237 guns lost. British casualties totalled 600 men. O'Connor's Desert Force, their spirits high, pushed on right through the Christmas period. Men had no time for celebration or festivities, and merely grabbed a hurried Christmas dinner of bully-beef as they squatted in the shade of their tanks.

Bardia was the next objective. Tanks stabbed through the defences at crack of dawn on 5th January, 1941, and infantrymen swarmed through the hole, turning to left and right as they streamed into the Italian positions. Long files of Italian prisoners stretched over the desert, shuffling back into captivity. Enemy hopes of invading Egypt were shattered.

General O'Connor continued to work miracles with the limited strength at his disposal. He had an uncanny knack of attacking from the least expected direction, and he continued to think ahead to the next move and the next, using his mobility to full advantage. Now Tobruk headed the list of targets. Already units of the 7th Armoured Division were streaking forward to surround this vital Mediterranean port, and British warships were concentrating offshore to pound the defences with their bombardment.

A legend is born

Land attacks against Tobruk, combined with the fierce air and naval bombardments, caused the town to surrender on 22nd January. One last target remained, and this the greatest of all – Benghazi, and the final, complete destruction of the entire Italian army in North Africa.

O'Connor and Wavell drew up their plans. The 7th Armoured Division, spearheaded by the 11th Hussars, would sweep left, outflanking the retreating Italian forces, and would block the coastal road on the far side of Benghazi at Beda Fomm. Meanwhile, the Australians would push forward along the coastal road to capture Benghazi itself. The Italians would thus be trapped from front and rear.

Such a plan sounds simple. In the confusion of battle, however, it appeared extremely complicated – and dangerous. The 11th Hussars had no maps of the area, and had to feel their way at top speed across the wilderness to Beda Fomm. They reached their objective, and sat astride the road on 5th February – just two hours before the first Italian troops approached. But the Hussar leader, Colonel John Combe, had only about 2,000 men with which to face more than 20,000 Italians.

For three hours the 11th Hussars and Rifle Brigade troops stood alone against Italian attacks. Time and again they refused to give ground. At last, over the horizon, came a swirl of dust – the leading tanks of the 4th Armoured Brigade. Their commander shouted one word over the radio: "Attack!" And the British battered into the left and rear of the leading Italian columns.

Only nightfall prevented an Italian defeat. Grimly, both sides continued to fight during the darkness, although the British remained heavily outnumbered. Next day the enemy attempted to break through

Below A map showing Wavell's advance from Sidi Barrani to El Agheila, which resulted in the collapse and surrender of the entire Italian army in North Africa (February, 1941).

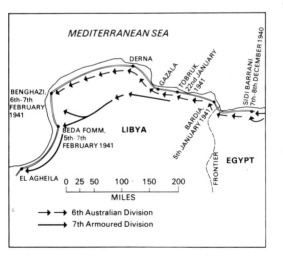

38

again and lost 100 tanks. And, that night, the Rifle Brigade withstood no less than nine frontal attacks. Still the British grip remained tight around the Italian throat. At dawn on 7th February, the enemy mustered all remaining tanks for one last push. This failed. The whole Italian army surrendered.

The desert and coastal road lay littered with smoking remains of tanks, guns, lorries, cars. The legend of the Desert Rats had been born.

Above Artillerymen carry out running repairs on their 4.5 gun before the battle starts up again.

3. Rommel

In two months, two solitary British divisions had advanced 500 miles, and destroyed an enemy army of ten divisions. Over 130,000 prisoners had been taken, and nearly 400 tanks and 800 guns.

The success had indeed been great. O'Connor later reported: "I think this may be termed a complete victory since none of the enemy escaped." His triumph remained unequalled by any other North African commander, German or British. And the way seemed open for the complete conquest of Tripolitania, up to the border of French Tunisia, before the German troops could arrive.

Unfortunately, despite this success, the British supply situation remained extremely weak. Any further advance would mean further difficulties in sending materials to the troops. Above all, the situation in North Africa was affected by the position elsewhere. Germany was preparing to invade Greece. German forces began to move through Hungary into Roumania early in January, 1941 – the attack on Greece was planned for the beginning of April. In London, Winston Churchill felt obliged to send help to this threatened ally. Yet this help could only come from the Middle East, which meant that British strength in North Africa was drastically reduced. Wavell had to order his forces to halt at El Agheila.

At the same time, Hitler decided to send troops to Tripolitania. And on Wednesday, 12th February, 1941, a senior German officer, described by a British reporter as "obscure," stepped onto Tripolitanian soil to command these troops. General Erwin Rommel had arrived.

Opposite As the British advanced into Libya, the supply situation became extremely weak, since their lines of communication stretched back over many treacherous miles. Here a driver snatches a few moments of rest, and a much-needed drink of water, before pressing on.

Unexpected attack

Rommel wrote: "Had Wavell continued his advance into Tripolitania [from Libya], no proper resistance could have been mounted against him." But Wavell reported to London: "I have to admit to taking considerable risks in Libya after the capture of Benghazi in order to provide maximum support for Greece."

The British were quite unaware of Rommel's skills, and did not believe he would start moving forward until May. Instead, Rommel prepared to strike at the end of March. "Speed is the thing that matters here," he wrote to his wife. On 24th March, 1941, the *Afrika Korps* made a small advance from Tripolitania to El Agheila on the Libyan border; yet still the High Command in Cairo refused to believe that Rommel would attempt a major assault. "I do not believe," signalled Wavell on the 30th, "that he can make any big effort for another month."

Next day, 31st March, the Desert Fox launched his full-scale, full-blooded attack. British outposts heard the squealing *Panzers* coming towards them; German aircraft streaked in to blast the Desert Rat positions. British units hurriedly pulled back or else were overrun. Wavell could only muster one armoured division, part of an infantry division and a motorized brigade to face the German onslaught. The Germans attacked with one *Panzer* division and two weak Italian divisions.

Rommel decided to defeat the Desert Rats with the same plan they themselves had used against the Italians, only this time in reverse. The 21st *Panzer* Division would strike across the Libyan desert towards Tobruk, while the Italian troops advanced along the coast road through Benghazi and on to Derna. From the very start, the Desert Rats had been thrown disastrously off-balance.

Opposite Rommel (on the left) discusses plans with one of his generals. Rommel was a great tactician, and believed in the necessity of swift and unexpected attack.

44

Rapid advance

"Dearest Lu," wrote Rommel to his wife on 3rd April. "We've been attacking since the 31st with dazzling success . . . "

Rommel's elation contrasted sharply with the depression felt by the Desert Rats. One commented: "Those days and nights were hellish. Sheer hell. We stumbled backwards. We couldn't find our feet. We couldn't take breath – and when we did we only got a lung-full of desert dust." The British 2nd Armoured Division, attempting to delay the enemy advance, found itself split. One brigade, forced into Derna through shortage of fuel, was captured on 6th April. Next day, most of the remainder of the division was surrounded and also forced to surrender.

And always Rommel drove his men forward, himself leading the advance. "Mechili clear of enemy," he signalled to his leading tanks. "Make for it. Drive fast. Rommel." So rapid was the enemy advance that when the prongs of Rommel's attack met at Mechili on 7th April, leading British generals were unable to flee from the trap in time. Two generals were captured – one of them the brilliant O'Connor.

These depressing reports from North Africa were matched by equally bad news from Greece. Troops taken from the desert to fight in the Grecian hills and valleys were outnumbered and almost overwhelmed. In attempting to do too much, in Greece and in North Africa, Britain now seemed in deadly danger of losing both.

The German commander turned his attention to the British forces still clinging to the most vital port of all along the North African shore – Tobruk.

Opposite Rommel liked to lead his *Panzer* divisions into battle himself, and was always in the forefront of any advance. Here he relaxes for a few minutes with the crew of a German tank, and discusses the day's work with them.

The clash at Tobruk

On 10th April, the Desert Fox told his staff that Egypt and the Suez Canal remained his objective, but that first Tobruk must be taken. The British, too, had realized just how important the port was – three days before, an Australian brigade had been moved by sea to strengthen the garrison. On 10th April, the 9th Australian Division arrived.

Rommel threw everything he had into the attack. His first main thrust against the Tobruk defences was launched in April. Both attackers and defenders tried frantically to strengthen their positions. General Morshead, the Australian commander, warned his men that they would never be allowed to surrender or to retreat: "There'll be no Dunkirk here. If we should have to get out, we shall have to fight our way out."

Rommel buzzed round the edge of the defences like an angry wasp, ordering his men to attack, attack, again and again. But the Australians refused to give ground. For three days and nights the battle raged. One soldier described the scene: "The brittle rasping and spitting of machine-guns; mortar-bombs flying over, whispering gently and crashing suddenly; solids blasting like express trains, leaving groaning, feverish turmoils of vacuum in their wake; and the mewing and squealing chorus of the 25-pounder shells as they arch over our heads."

German Stuka dive-bombers screamed in to blast the Australian positions, and the bombs sent up great gusts of dust, most of them with angry, ugly black centres telling of hits on vehicles or houses. For their part, the defenders relied upon the massive British warships, lying offshore, which continually

pounded the German attackers with their powerful long-range guns. By night the whole skyline, land and sea, remained lit by flashing, searing explosions, and the air throbbed with the thudding bombardment. Australian troops sagged with weariness, covered with dust and filth and wringing wet with sweat, with no possibility of relief or rest.

Yet still the Tobruk defences held.

Above A British sentry stands guard above the wire defences on the outskirts of Tobruk (1941). Both the Germans and the British realized the vital strategic importance of Tobruk, and the battle for it was long and hard.

Stalemate

Rommel's attack failed. Two more attempts were made in April; both were repulsed. By 2nd May, the Desert Fox accepted that "we were not strong enough to mount the large-scale attack necessary to take the fortress." The Australians had won their victory and their fame. They remained surrounded, but triumphant; and the port stayed in Allied hands for the next eight critical months.

Rommel's setback at Tobruk even led to doubts among the German High Command as to his ability. Halder, Hitler's military chief in Berlin,

Below Despite repeated German attacks, the port of Tobruk remained in Allied hands. Here a British infantryman sits on guard on the ramparts outside the town. Notice the mascot painted on his helmet.

believed him to be "stark mad." He wrote: "Reports from officers coming home from the area show that Rommel is in no way equal to his task. He spends the whole day rushing about between widely-scattered units . . . and fritters away his forces."

The Desert Fox, however, was in a delicate position. His forces had to continue to surround Tobruk and keep the garrison at bay, and this reduced the strength and ability of the *Afrika Korps* to pursue the Desert Rats. A further German advance into Egypt now seemed impossible, and Rommel had to content himself with holding a line just across the frontier, stretching from Sollum on the coast to Sidi Omar further inland. His supply problem was by now serious.

Yet neither had the Desert Rats much cause for optimism. They too could only manage to find a skeleton force with which to hold the frontier. Wavell remained anxious about Greece, and also had to deal with fighting in Abyssinia. Trouble had broken out in Iraq, and the Germans looked like intervening in Syria. British forces were evacuated from Greece to Crete. On 20th May, the island suffered a terrible German onslaught. Eleven days later, the surviving British units had to be rescued.

Once again, both sides in the desert war tried to reinforce faster than the other. And Wavell received a boost from London: at Churchill's insistence, more than 300 tanks were sent by convoy direct through the Mediterranean, instead of by the longer, but safer, sea-route round South Africa and up the Suez Canal. These valuable weapons arrived in May. Churchill wanted the Desert Rats to use them in an attack as soon as possible.

C

"Battleaxe"

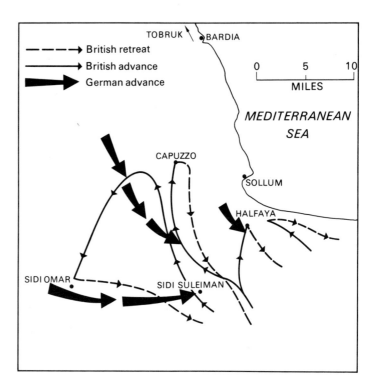

Right A plan of operation "Battleaxe" – Wavell's attempt to relieve Tobruk, which failed when Rommel's swift counter-attack threw the Desert Rats into confusion (June, 1941).

"There is battle in the air," wrote an experienced Desert Rat officer. "I swear there is. It lies thick on the tongue."

Because of political pressure from home, Wavell was now forced to push forward and attempt to relieve Tobruk. The operation was given the code-name "Battleaxe." Despite the arrival of the Mediterranean convoy, however, his resources were still extremely meagre. The Middle East Command would probably have waited longer before attacking, had not Churchill been exerting such pressure on them to attack immediately.

50

Early on Saturday, 14th June, 1941, Wavell signalled to General Beresford-Peirse, now commanding the Desert Rats: " 'Battleaxe' is the most important operation yet undertaken in the Middle East . . . " Late on the Saturday afternoon, British tanks began to move forward, aiming at the German forces holding the positions along the Egyptian frontier. They hoped to catch them by surprise, but Rommel was expecting them. His forces had been alerted and, although British units took Capuzzo, the important Halfaya pass remained in German hands.

"Today – it's 2.30 in the morning – will see the decision," wrote Rommel to his wife on the 16th. "It's going to be a hard fight, so you'll understand why I can't sleep." Once more Rommel showed his brilliance, and confounded his critics. One *Panzer* attack broke through the 7th Armoured Division; Rommel hastily prepared a second thrust, ordering it forward to threaten the Desert Rats with encirclement. And once again the British were thrown off-balance. The *Panzers* battered onwards throughout the night of the 16th; by dawn they had started to draw together within striking distance of Halfaya, cutting communications to the Desert Rats out in front. The British commanders, bewildered, began to lose control. Rommel accelerated the advance; and the Desert Rats had to retreat in order to avoid the trap.

Wavell signalled to Churchill: "I regret to report failure of 'Battleaxe.' " But the Germans, as well as the British, had suffered heavy tank casualties. Both sides could do little more than stay in their present positions.

Above A British soldier scrambles up a rocky hillside to get a better view of the battle below.

Auchinleck's attempt

The failure of "Battleaxe," and Churchill's disappointment, led to Wavell's replacement by Auchinleck on 1st July. Almost immediately strong pressure was put upon the new Middle East commander to start another offensive. But Auchinleck refused to be hurried. Neither did Rommel listen to pleas from Berlin and Rome to push on into Egypt. Both commanders decided instead to build up their respective strengths. The Western Desert Force was renamed the 8th Army, and was reinforced to seven divisions and 700 tanks. Rommel had just over 400 tanks, and it would be difficult for him to obtain further supplies – Hitler had invaded Russia, and needed all available forces for this new Eastern Front.

On 18th November, the Desert Rats attacked. For days past, troops had been transferred to the forward areas; supply lines had been improved; bombing of enemy positions at Halfaya, Sidi Omar and Sollum had been increased. One eye-witness wrote in his diary: "The push is on. We moved up last night after dark and a few miles short of the [frontier] wire went into a very shrouded leaguer [temporary defensive position]. We weren't even allowed to light a cigarette.

"This morning we rose at four in pitch dark, and at first streak of dawn are off. And so apparently are all the other units of our armoured division, as though released in some gigantic race . . . As far as the eye can reach over the desert face are dust-reeking lines of vehicles – pennanted tanks and armoured cars, guns and limbers, carriers, trucks and lorries – all speeding along in parallel course westwards to Libya."

Auchinleck's attack, "Crusader," had been launched just five days before Rommel intended to attack Tobruk. The Desert Fox was taken by surprise, and the British advance continued largely unopposed throughout the 18th. The lack of opposition, however, led to a serious British mistake. The next day, overconfident, yet puzzled by the absence of the enemy, General Cunningham allowed his forces to split up. But, by now, Rommel was aware of the threat.

Vicious fighting erupted along the whole line. Tanks milled in the desert, charging, reforming, charging again. By 21st November, the Desert Rats and the *Afrika Korps* were locked in the fiercest tank fighting seen in the whole North African campaign.

Opposite British troops, stripped to the waist, dig a gun-pit in the desert for an anti-aircraft gun.

Below A plan of Auchinleck's attack, "Crusader." At first, all went well for the British, and they advanced without opposition. But then, over-confident, they allowed their forces to split up and, at Sidi Rezegh, the German *Panzers* struck back (November, 1941).

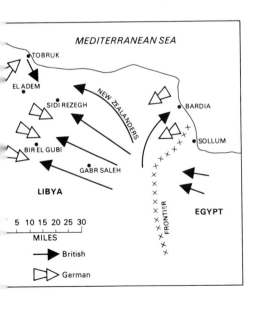

Auchinleck to the rescue

Burned and twisted tanks piled up on the blackened sand. So close together were the opposing sides that the R.A.F. could barely distinguish between them. "Time meant nothing," a Desert Rat tank commander remembered. "We just went on, firing, manoeuvring, frantically trying to avoid presenting a target. Two tanks on either side of me went up with a massive roar, almost together. The crews were fried alive."

"It looks as if the battle is moving to its climax," signalled Auchinleck to London on the 23rd. The day, a Sunday, dawned with thick mist shrouding the battlefield. The *Afrika Korps* slashed forward to the important positions south of Sidi-Rezegh and, despite terrible casualties, gradually battered a bloody way forward. By nightfall the area defenders, the South African Brigade, had lost 3,394 men, and were almost wiped out.

Panzers now commanded this section of the battlefield; Rommel believed that the British were about to collapse, and so split his forces in order to forge ahead towards Egypt, in the hope of cutting off the Desert Rats' retreat. British defeat seemed inevitable.

But Auchinleck, flying to the forward H.Q. during the afternoon, believed otherwise. New Zealand troops were working their way round to join up with the Tobruk garrison; Rommel's casualties were almost as great as those suffered by the Desert Rats, and the Desert Fox would tire his remaining tanks by a useless thrust towards Egypt. If the Desert Rats stood firm, avoided panic and regrouped, Rommel would have to return to deal with this threat from the rear. So Auchinleck mastered the slipping

Opposite The aftermath of battle – wrecks of tanks litter the desert sand.
Below A map of the battle at Sidi-Rezegh, showing how Rommel thrust towards Egypt in the hope of cutting off the British retreat, and was then forced to retrace his steps in order to protect his own rear. By the beginning of December, 1941, the *Afrika Korps* had retreated back to its original position.

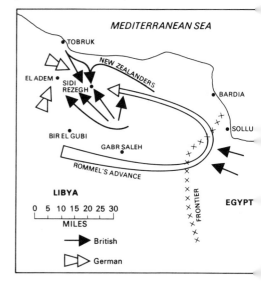

situation. The absence of the main bulk of the enemy on 25th and 26th November allowed the exhausted Desert Rats to pull themselves together. Then Rommel was forced to return from his futile dash towards Egypt, which had considerably weakened his striking power.

Further terrible fighting took place on the 29th and 30th, and Rommel regained some ground. But his two *Panzer* divisions had only about 40 tanks left between them. At the beginning of December, the *Afrika Korps* had once more to retreat to its original position at El Agheila.

Rommel replies

But the pendulum of fortune swung back again. This time it was the turn of the Desert Rats to suffer from overstretched supplies, as they reached across Egypt and Libya towards El Agheila. The 8th Army was only able to savour victory for one short month. During the weeks of winter, the British suffered severe naval losses in the Mediterranean. And, in the Far East, the Japanese entered the war, sinking the battleships *Prince of Wales* and *Repulse*. Naval shortages reduced supplies to the 8th Army.

Once again Rommel felt confident enough to prepare for another, unexpected, stroke. He wrote to his wife on 17th January: "I'm full of plans that I daren't say anything about round here. They'd think me crazy." And, on 21st January, Rommel added: "The army launches its counter-attack in two hours' time. After carefully weighing the pros and cons, I've decided to take the risk. I have complete faith that God is keeping a protective hand over us and that He will grant us victory."

On 21st January, 1942, two *Panzer* columns knifed forward to take advantage of the unprepared British defences. Ritchie, the 8th Army Commander, completely misjudged the situation. He thought Rommel had merely launched a strong scouting party. Desert Rat units at the front, however, soon realized how mistaken their commander had been. Wave after wave of *Panzer* charges washed against the British positions during the 23rd and 24th; by 25th January, the 8th Army line had begun to crack. Rommel was vindicated. The log-book of the 15th *Panzer* Division noted that the tanks "broke into the enemy at a tearing speed and threw him into complete confusion."

Below It was very important for the Desert Rats to keep in touch with what was happening, not only in North Africa but in the whole world. They even had their own newspaper, *The Eighth Army News,* as shown in this picture.

Rommel handled his columns with superb confidence. He launched dummy attacks, manoeuvred, struck swiftly in the most unexpected places, maintained the pressure, and generated panic among the Desert Rats. Back they tumbled to Gazala.

All possible reinforcements were scraped together and shoved forward. Gradually, at Gazala, the 8th Army established a defensive line. Rommel, short of fuel, paused to regroup. And, for four months, both sides prepared for the decisive battle.

Below During pauses in the battle, both sides hurried to repair the damaged tanks and guns. The British soldiers in this picture are working in a makeshift blacksmith's shop, hammering out broken machinery.

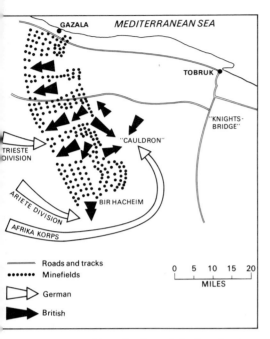

Roads and tracks
Minefields
German
British

0 5 10 15 20
MILES

GAZALA
MEDITERRANEAN SEA
TOBRUK
"KNIGHTS-BRIDGE"
"CAULDRON"
TRIESTE DIVISION
ARIETE DIVISION
AFRIKA KORPS
BIR HACHEIM

Above A plan of the battle at Gazala, showing how Rommel managed to sweep round to the south of the British position, and make the British minefields part of his own defences (June, 1942).

Opposite This British soldier on look-out patrol has made himself quite comfortable with sandbags.

Turmoil at Gazala

British positions stretched from Gazala near the coast to Bir Hacheim in the desert to the south. Rommel had a simple plan. He would overcome the British flank at Bir Hacheim, and then roll up the Desert Rat line from south to north.

His tanks began to creep forward during the night of 26th May, past dim lights concealed in petrol cans – these were placed to indicate the line of march south round the British positions. The full German advance began soon after midnight. The Italian *Ariete* Division had been ordered to take Bir Hacheim itself, while the Italian *Trieste* Division stabbed at the centre of the British line further north. This would leave the *Afrika Korps* free to sweep south-east round Bir Hacheim to strike at the rear of the British defences, while the *Panzers* moved in the direction of Tobruk.

When the main battle began next morning, 27th May, the Desert Rats were once again caught off-guard. The southern sweep by the *Afrika Korps* threw their defences into confusion, although French defenders managed to drive the Italians from Bir Hacheim itself. While this position remained in Allied hands, the British could pose a serious threat to the *Afrika Korps* supply lines.

But Desert Rat tanks were being wasted in small, unlinked efforts, while Rommel kept his *Panzers* in a tight, deadly mass. Fierce fighting throughout the 28th resulted in heavy losses on both sides. Rommel's *Panzer* groups gradually drew together in the area behind the British line – this area, scene of great turmoil, would afterwards be known as "The Cauldron."

Just as Rommel was about to run out of petrol,

the *Trieste* Division managed to break through the minefields to open up a new supply route. Rommel shifted into these minefields in the centre of the British line, and plugged the gaps behind him with strong anti-tank artillery. In this way, the British minefields became part of Rommel's own defences.

Desert Rat units tried to force their way through to their surrounded allies at Bir Hacheim, without success. "The Stukas are still dropping masses of muck," wrote one of the soldiers involved in these rescue attempts. "Rumour suggests the situation inside Bir Hacheim is getting a bit desperate."

Right A French soldier who
survived the continuous
bombardment at Bir Hacheim
is escorted, shirtless but still
carrying his greatcoat and
rifle, back to the British lines
(June, 1942).

Flight into Egypt

The rumours were correct. On 10th June, this same
soldier wrote in his diary: "Tonight is the end of
Bir Hacheim . . . From now on, it's bedlam – rat-
tatting of machine guns, crashing of mortars, hoarse
rumbling of shells, white, red and green lights
climbing at all angles into the sky, streams of white
and yellow tracer playing over the horizon, sprouting
red glows, and all the while the drone and surge of
vehicle engines."

Surviving Frenchmen at Bir Hacheim attempted

to break through the ring to freedom. "When there's sufficient light, single men and small bands approach furtively, and recognizing us, join us. They're haggard, unshaven, tattered and tired, but one after another, on the instinct of discipline, gripping weapons and equipment, they fall into rank."

With Bir Hacheim fallen, and the threat to his communications removed, Rommel was free to stab forward again. He concentrated his attacks on the position in the centre of the battle area, known as Knightsbridge. During the night of 13th June, the occupying Guards Brigade was forced to withdraw with heavy tank losses. Rommel was left in control of the battlefield.

The 8th Army began to quicken its withdrawal back into Egypt. On 21st June, 1942, Winston Churchill, then visiting Washington, was handed a pink slip of paper containing the terrible news – Tobruk had been taken by the Germans. For the first and only time in the Second World War, staff officers saw the Prime Minister wince with pain.

Auchinleck rushed forward to take over personal command of the fleeing Desert Rats. On 28th June, he attempted to rally the troops at Mersa Matruh, but once again the Desert Rats had to pull back. On 1st July, Rommel threw his forces forward, urging all possible speed. The Desert Rats scrambled into new defensive positions. Nearby lay a small, scruffy Arab village, with a name which would soon become famous – El Alamein. On 2nd July, the *Afrika Korps* attempted to smash through this new line, only 80 miles from Alexandria. But Auchinleck showed himself to be a cool, skilled and courageous commander, and the line held. The Desert Rats had been brought nearer total defeat than ever before, but had been saved at the last minute.

4. Montgomery

Prospects for the Desert Rats still seemed dim in the late summer of 1942. Rommel's advance had been a brilliant display of tank leadership. The disaster had cost the British 75,000 casualties, including the 33,000 garrison of Tobruk. Defeat also cost Auchinleck his command in the Middle East. Both he and the actual 8th Army commander, Ritchie, were sacked in August. General Harold Alexander took over from Auchinleck in Cairo, while General Bernard Montgomery became the new 8th Army commander.

"Monty" arrived in the battle area at a time of grave danger, and immediately made plans to strengthen the defences at Alamein. The situation was extremely perilous. The enemy remained at the doors of Alexandria and Cairo. Panic swept these teeming cities, and many rich Egyptians seriously considered fleeing the country. Secret papers were stacked ready for burning should the Germans arrive. Many people believed that if only Rommel could summon strength for one more push, total victory would be his.

But these fears were proved unjustified. The Desert Rats still had plenty of fight left in them. Moreover, their supply lines were now short, while Rommel's stretched back far across the desert wasteland.

German stores were running low. Montgomery rightly believed that the enemy would be unable to stand a long battle, because in doing so they would use up all their precious petrol, ammunition and even water. The British commander made his plans, while the Desert Rats tried to snatch brief rests before the coming conflict.

Opposite A camera portrait of "Monty" wearing typical battle-dress.

The pleasures of Cairo

Some Desert Rats had been in North Africa for as much as six years. And the only real relief they could obtain from the fighting and from the desert was to be found in Cairo, or perhaps in Alexandria.

Cairo bustled with soldiers, sailors and airmen. Troops from many different countries jostled in the narrow, smelly streets and in the smoky, stifling bars. Egyptian taxi-drivers, barmen, café owners, fly-whisk sellers, shopkeepers – all did a thriving trade. The more successful the 8th Army was, the friendlier the Egyptians became. When reports from the desert seemed depressing, as in the early autumn of 1942, the local people started to learn German and Italian, ready for a possible enemy takeover.

For the ordinary soldiers, these short spells of leave meant a chance to sleep in reasonable comfort. So they slept long hours, and enjoyed huge meals of steak and chips, eggs, milk-shakes, ice-cream, lemonade – and plenty of beer. Boisterous singing bellowed from the bars, as the troops bawled out their favourite marching songs. Less noisy celebrations took place at the numerous clubs established

Below A view of the Shepheard's Hotel in Cairo, a favourite haunt of Desert Rat officers on leave.

for the troops, such as the Y.M.C.A., the Empire, the New Zealand and the Tipperary. Men relaxed at the cinema, or toured the Pyramids, pestered by a host of would-be guides.

The officers were made even more comfortable. They could enjoy the luxury of the plush Shepheard's Hotel, or the Continental, and dress up in their best uniforms. Young officers of the 11th Hussars, with their cherry coloured tight-fitting trousers, sauntered proudly over the thick carpets. A multitude of badges glittered from the caps in the cloakrooms. More senior officers might receive invitations from high-ranking Egyptians to sample the delights of the expensive Mahomed Ali Club, or they might attend garden parties in the cool green gardens of the rich suburb of Gezireh.

But for all of them, both officers and men, leave could last no more than 14 days. Then would come a hurried trip to buy presents to send home – trinkets, alabaster pots and vases, leatherwork, statuettes . . . And once again the desert lay ahead, and the prospect of battle.

Left A typical Cairo back street, where British soldiers could wander through the flies and dust to buy souvenirs for their families, and forget about the battle that lay ahead.

Preparations

General Montgomery introduced himself to his troops, and visited each unit in turn. One Desert Rat described his arrival at the camp: "He proves to be a quiet, severe sort of chap, smallish but tough, with a short moustache, pointed features.

"The inspection lasts a long while, but the General . . . holds it in a steady grip, moving slowly along the ranks, methodically scrutinizing each man – up from the boots, then shooting a quizzical glance at the face with a sudden upward lunge of his head."

Rommel knew he would have to act soon. British strength grew daily, while his own forces became weaker. On 31st August, he lunged forward into the attack. The Desert Fox attempted the same plan which he had used so successfully at Gazala – outflanking the British line to the south, then striking behind the British positions. But Montgomery was prepared. He was woken up at the start of the battle. "Excellent," he declared, supremely confident, and went straight back to sleep again.

German *Panzers* striking south were delayed by 7th Armoured Division units, then found themselves up against a solid mass of Desert Rat tanks, which were dug in at the vital Alam Halfa ridge to the rear of the main British positions. This ridge at Alam Halfa served the same purpose as Bir Hacheim had done at Gazala, and posed a severe threat to the German communication lines. Rommel had to sacrifice his strength in attempts to storm the Desert Rat positions.

The German retreat began on 3rd September. Montgomery decided to let Rommel retire, since he wanted to keep the 8th Army intact for the decisive

Below A plan of the battle at the Alam Halfa ridge, where German *Panzer* divisions relentlessly attacked, and relentlessly were repulsed. After three days of fierce conflict, the Germans were finally forced to retreat (3rd September, 1942).

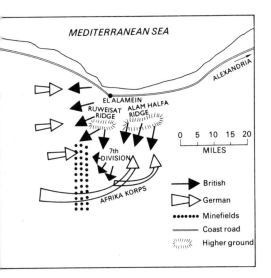

Above Montgomery was in no hurry to launch his big offensive, and spent many weeks in preparation. Here British troops on "alarm" rush from their tents during an exercise.

battle of Alamein. The Desert Fox hurriedly built a defensive minefield, but he knew that his desert reign was almost done.

Montgomery, however, took his time. Dummy tanks were placed in the desert to confuse the enemy, and preparations increased during October. "Training is strenuous," wrote one British soldier, "and there are many signs of approaching action. All the other camps in the area are now filled with infantry, tank and artillery units."

The battle of Alamein

The battle of Alamein was a terrible slogging match. Montgomery aimed to punch two holes through the enemy's minefields, using infantry to clear a way through. Tanks could then pour along the corridors and sweep into the open desert behind the enemy positions.

At 9.40 p.m. on 23rd October, 1942, about 1,000 British guns opened a mighty bombardment against the enemy defences. "The guns nearby crash incessantly," wrote an eyewitness in his diary, "searing the darkness with gashes of flame, and those farther up and down the line rumble wrathfully and convulse the northern and southern horizons with ceaseless flashing and flickering. Groups of Jock [Scottish] infantry, in shorts and tin-hats, with bayonets fixed, begin filtering forward . . . Poor devils – I don't envy them their work."

One soldier waiting to move into the attack found time to write: "I look straight up into the face of the moon, which is waxen and pallid and wears an expression, so it seems to me, of incredulous dismay at the fantastic scene being enacted down here on this patch of earth." Ghastly fighting continued next day, amidst the stench of cordite, smoke and sweat. Bodies lay heaped on the sand, the flies buzzing black around them. Men became crazed with fear and thirst.

Montgomery had to halt the southern attempt to crash through the minefield, and instead switched the main thrust to the north, near the vital coastal road. Men of the 9th Australian Division battled forward in the swirling black smoke; nearby New Zealanders also thrust forward.

"A regiment is going by in single file as I scribble this on the back of a message-form pad," wrote a Desert Rat. "Each tank has its name on the side,

Below A plan of what Montgomery aimed to do at Alamein – to punch two corridors through the German minefield, along which the tanks could pour into the open desert behind the enemy positions.

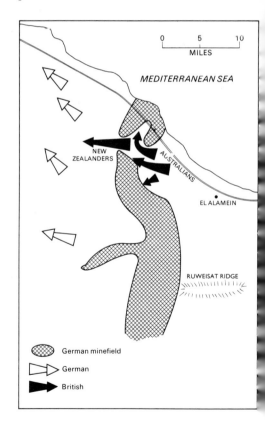

68

below the turret – *Ajax, Agincourt, Audacious, Attila, Argonaut, Achilles, Ark Royal, Adamant,* and so on, lurching and grinding, and making a terrific din.'' Within minutes many of those tanks would be blackened, burning coffins.

After a week of bloody slaughter, British strength began to tell. Rommel's last reserves were hurled into the fight. On 1st November, he had to shift back slightly. And Montgomery prepared for the final onslaught – operation "Supercharge."

Below Hammered by British artillery, German troops shelter in the sand, while the explosion of a shell not far away raises a blinding cloud of dust and smoke. Under such conditions, men soon became crazed with fear and thirst.

69

Operation "Supercharge"

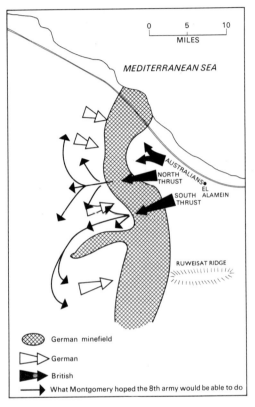

0   5   10
MILES

MEDITERRANEAN SEA

AUSTRALIANS
NORTH
THRUST
EL
ALAMEIN
SOUTH ALAMEIN
THRUST

RUWEISAT RIDGE

German minefield

German

British

What Montgomery hoped the 8th army would be able to do

Above A plan of operation "Supercharge," Monty's final thrust through the German minefields which led to the rout of the *Afrika Korps* (2nd November, 1942).

The Desert Rats launched the final push at 1 a.m. on Monday, 2nd November, 1942. All day the infantry fought forward to clear a way through the minefield for the tanks. One infantryman described what it was like as he waited for another move forward: "It's most unpleasant crouching in the bottom of the pit, packed tight with still more chaps whose single object is to keep their 'nuts' down as low as possible, silently braced and wondering whether the next shell is coming our way.

"Shells scream down in inexorable succession, and all around us is the driving, rending crash of high explosives. Several times my tin-hat is crushed onto my head by the impact . . . Everyone lies still."

This particular group of Desert Rats wiped out thirty-seven German tanks. And, under this type of pressure, the *Afrika Korps* began at last to crack. More and more *Panzers* lay crippled in the blazing battlefield. Desert Rat tanks ground forward, messages passing from one to another over the short-range radio. This conversation was recorded by an eyewitness:

" 'Hallo 11. Can you find out what's going on in front of you?'

'Sorry Angus. Can't see a damn thing.'

'Hallo 15. Just tell George to move over to his right a bit. I don't seem to get him from here . . . '

'Afraid I don't get him either, Angus. His set must be U.S.'

'Hallo 8. There's something over on my left. I can't quite make out what. Looks like a row of funny little squat, square things.'

"Suddenly there's a colossal whoosh-bang, and a

70

sheet of flame leaps across the darkness ahead. Then another tremendous crash. My heart freezes. Those 'funny little squat square things' are obviously Jerry anti-tank guns . . . A voice bellows urgently over the intercom: 'For Christ's sake, *get spread out!*' "

During the night of 2nd November, the tanks at last reach the desert beyond the German positions. The enemy lines have been pierced. Desert Rats streak out into the open. Rommel and his *Afrika Korps* begin to retreat.

Above German soldiers crouch behind the shelter of a small ridge during the fierce fighting at Alamein. The battle was exceptionally tough for infantrymen on both sides.

71

Retreating hosts

"We crawl along in fits and starts," wrote a Desert Rat during the pursuit, "with Sherman tanks, endless files of them, hemming us in, churning up thick clouds of sand, and filling the air ceaselessly with the clamour of their engines . . . I'm smothered in sand. On every side the desert is smoking densely, reeking up to the wan stars. I develop a terrific thirst, which I try to assuage with frequent guzzles of warm, stale water from the hot cans on board and immediately sweat it out in sticky sandpaste."

Back rolled the remains of the *Afrika Korps*; on swept the Desert Rats. Rommel's strength had been

Below A detachment of Italian soldiers, refugees from Alamein, race across the desert towards the shelter of a small town on their long retreat westwards

Above British anti-aircraft gunners stand ready for action.

cut by about a half – he had started the battle with 100,000 men, and had suffered 20,000 killed and 30,000 taken prisoner. Nearly 1,000 guns and over 400 tanks had been left on the battlefield. The 8th Army had lost 13,500 men killed, wounded or missing. About 100 guns had been destroyed and 500 tanks rendered unfit for further fighting.

"The coast road, over to our right, is all night overhung with smoky orange flares, presumably dropped by our aircraft on Jerry's retreating hosts."

Rommel's iron discipline still exerted control over these "retreating hosts." He made a delaying stand at Mersa Matruh on 7th November, and his troops fought bravely until they were forced back again through lack of fuel and ammunition. The *Afrika Korps* retreated over the Egyptian frontier into Libya, past the frontier wire and the rusty remains of previous battles, and past the shallow graves of comrades who had fallen earlier in the year.

Montgomery issued a message to the Desert Rats: "Today, 12th November, there are no German and Italian soldiers on Egyptian territory except prisoners. In three weeks we have completely smashed the German and Italian army, and pushed the fleeing remnants out of Egypt. And we have advanced ourselves nearly 300 miles up to and beyond the frontier." But Montgomery added: "Our task is not finished yet; the Germans are out of Egypt but there are still some left farther west, in Libya; and our leading troops are now in Libya ready to begin another assault.

"And this time, having reached Benghazi and beyond, we shall not come back. On with the task, and good hunting to you all . . . "

The race for Tunisia

After Libya, the 8th Army marched into Tripolitania and Tunisia. But, by now, they had help, coming from the opposite end of North Africa. Massive American and British landings had taken place in the French North African territories of Morocco and Algeria. The invasion, codenamed "Torch," passed off successfully on 8th November, and the troops were now moving through Algeria towards Tunisia. The Desert Rats were also thrusting into Tunisia from the other side, by way of Tripolitania. The enemy would soon be trapped in-between. The race for Tunis, the final objective, had begun.

But Montgomery was forced to ease pressure for the moment, and he turned aside to reopen the port of Benghazi and to rest his weary troops. The Desert Rats had now advanced over 1,200 miles, and the usual problems of finding supplies had begun.

Despite these difficulties, Montgomery ordered the pursuit to begin again early in January, 1943. He told his troops: "The leading units of the 8th Army are now only about 200 miles from Tripoli. The enemy is between us and the port, and they hope to hold us off. *The 8th Army is going to Tripoli . . .* Nothing can stop us."

The desert-hardened 8th Army slammed forward again on 15th January. Within a week the enemy had been thrown back. Desert Rats entered Tripoli at 4 a.m. on 23rd January, 1943, three months to a day since the beginning of the Alamein battle. Ahead loomed Tunisia.

News of these successes inflamed the people at home with a new enthusiasm. At last a British army had thrashed a powerful German force. These words, written at the time, show just how much hero-worship the Desert Rats evoked: "Libya is full of our troops. It is grand. Everywhere there are eager

Left American airmen, members of the "Torch" invasion force, study the map before making a sortie.
Below left A map showing how the German army in North Africa was gradually trapped between the twin advances of the British 8th Army from the east, and the "Torch" troops from the west.

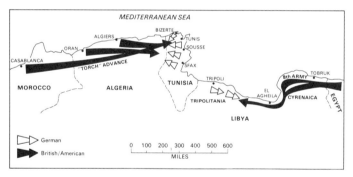

faces; convoy commanders sitting up aloft in their trucks like sunburned gods – their sun compasses pointing a black sliver of shadow towards the Boche [Germans]; despatch riders bumping incredibly through the sandy, rutted tracks; officers in groups, maps on knees, listening to their orders; lorried infantry waiting, waiting, waiting; guns, their dust covers off, marching through the infantry and off to a flank in majestic indifference."

Winter stalemate

Yet stern trials still lay ahead, both for the "Torch" invasion troops under General Eisenhower and for the 8th Army itself under Montgomery, before North Africa was finally cleared of enemy forces.

Eisenhower's army met fierce resistance as it advanced from the west through Algeria. American tank crews found themselves outmatched by the heavier, more powerful *Panzers*. This account describes a duel between an American tank, driven by a young lieutenant, Daubin, and a German adversary: "The German tank shed sparks like a power-driven grindstone. Yet he came on, 150 yards away, then 100 and 75. In a frenzy of desperation and fading faith in his highly-touted weapon, Daubin pumped more than 18 rounds at the German tank which continued to rumble towards him . . . Daubin could see the tracers hit, then glance straight up — popcorn balls, he thought, thrown by Little Bo Peep. Fifty yards away, Jerry paused. Daubin sensed what was coming and braced himself.

"The German loosed a round that screamed like an under-nourished banshee. The shell ricochetted off the wadi bank a trifle short, and showered sand and gravel into Daubin's open turret hatch." Daubin hastily attempted to retreat. "He climbed into his turret and straightened up for a quick look out of the open hatch. At that moment, death, inexplicably deferred, struck. The slug that was doubtlessly aimed at the turret struck the vertical surface of the armoured doors and caved in the front of the tank. The driver was instantly killed. Blown out of the turret by the concussion, Daubin was thrown to the ground . . . "

This type of combat took place time and again

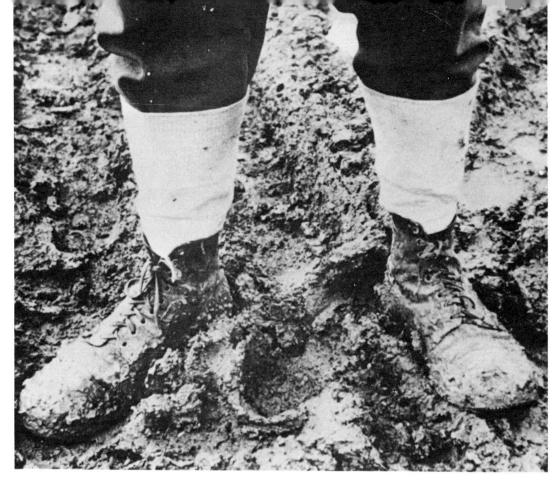

Above The winter rains turned the upper crust of Tunisia into a sea of mud, and hampered the Allied advance.

throughout Eisenhower's arduous advance. He could only proceed very cautiously – roads had to be made wider, and bridges stronger, to allow the use of his heavier tanks.

British and American units from the "Torch" landings managed to reach within 20 miles of Tunis at the beginning of December. But then came the winter rains, turning roads into quagmires, bogging down lorries and even tanks, and forcing men to wade knee-deep in mud. Rains also affected the flow of supplies to the Desert Rats. And gales in the Mediterranean hindered naval convoys carrying essential material to North Africa. The race for Tunis slowed, and finally halted. Winter stalemate set in.

5. Victory

When Winston Churchill visited the Desert Rats in February, 1943, he told them: "Ever since your victory at Alamein, you have nightly pitched your moving tents a day's march nearer home." Home really meant Tunis. With the capture of Tunisia would come the final defeat of German and Italian troops in North Africa, now led jointly by General von Arnim and Rommel, the weary Desert Fox.

Both sides prepared for the last campaign, and the rains continued to sluice down on the sodden troops. Back in England, this delay brought fresh gloom. But the British and American commanders could only wait until the black clouds rolled away from the Tunisian skies and the ground became firm enough for the tanks to grind forward.

The Desert Rats tried to scratch comfort from their inhospitable surroundings. They made little homes, or "bivvies," from whatever materials they could find – tents, packing cases, discarded crates, petrol tins. "I've grown quite attached to my little private bivvy," wrote one soldier. "It's so small you have to crawl in on your belly, but what a pleasant sanctuary it is!

"Inside, there's just enough room for my bed, packs, rifle, wireless-kit and several piles of books . . . The floor is covered with cardboard from petrol-tin packing cases." From his doorway the soldier could admire the desert view – "foreground of hard sand and stones; middle distance of grassy hummocks, scrub-bushes, and a myriad nodding, lemon-coloured wild flowers, and a far horizon of brown hills."

These flowers revealed that spring was approaching. And soon the "bivvies" would have to be taken apart, and belongings packed. The 8th Army, and the "Torch" troops over in the west, would be on the move again.

Opposite Two British soldiers get down to domestic tasks, ironing and darning, in the privacy of their "bivvy." As the picture shows, these improvised shelters could be made quite homelike.

Attack at Kasserine

Once again, however, it was the incredible Rommel who struck first, in a desperate attempt to shatter British and American plans. Leaving a small force to hold the 8th Army at the border of Tunisia in the east, he rapidly shifted units across to stab at Eisenhower's positions in the west. Rommel wanted to launch a two-fisted attack – first he would hit the Americans and British in the west, then he would turn round to give Montgomery and his Desert Rats a final blow in the face at Mareth.

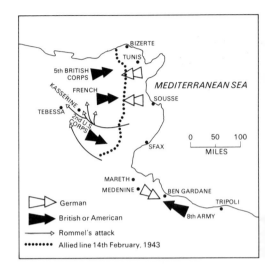

So, on St. Valentine's Day, 14th February, 1943, the Germans struck westwards against the thinly-spread and unprepared "Torch" troops. To begin with, all went well for the enemy. A German tank commander described the advance: "I was rounding a sharp curve when I sighted and recognized a Sherman tank on the road ahead, within attacking range. I jerked the wheel in the driver's hand and the vehicle swerved sharply . . .

"The detachment manning the gun immediately behind me were swift in taking their cue. In a matter of seconds they had jumped from their seats, un-limbered, swung round and fired their first shell . . . It struck the tank at an angle in the flank. The tank burst into flames. We probed ahead and soon ran into fire from tanks and machine-guns deployed on either side of the road . . . Steady fighting went on for an hour. Then thick columns of black smoke rose ahead, followed by explosions . . . The enemy tanks ceased firing. We continued to advance . . ."

Rommel's *Panzers* crashed through the Kasserine Pass on 18th February and fanned northwards. But resistance against Rommel steadily increased in the

mountainous countryside. The Americans and British fought back with ever-mounting strength, while Rommel's slender supplies fast dwindled. And the joint German commander, von Arnim, did not give him much support. "Valuable time was being squandered," wrote Rommel. "I was extremely angry." In the end, not even his skill and energy could prevent the failure of the offensive. By 23rd February, his tanks had begun to pull back. A secondary attack, launched by von Arnim on 26th February, also proved unsuccessful. And Rommel now saw the hideous spectre of total destruction rising before him.

Above A detachment of American troops shelter under an overhanging shelf, waiting for the chance to attack an unsuspecting German tank.

Opposite A map showing how Rommel, trapped by the advancing Allied forces, intended to attack first in the west against the "Torch" troops at Kasserine, and then in the east against the British 8th Army at Mareth and Medenine (March, 1943).

81

Medenine and Mareth

Yet stubborn Rommel still refused to admit defeat. On 6th March, he switched his attention back to the Desert Rats at Medenine, and launched an attack with two armoured and two infantry divisions in a final despairing fling.

The Desert Rats were well prepared in excellent defensive positions. One officer described what happened: "They were a mixed bag of Germans in the khaki uniforms of the *Afrika Korps* and Italians in their dark green tunics. They advanced by sections in close formation, and offered an admirable target. I took over a Bren gun myself, and shouting to the others to hold their fire, waited until they

Above General Cunningham (on the left) and his commander Montgomery pose outside their tent headquarters before the final attack.

Opposite A captured German 8-wheeled armoured car is strapped onto a lorry for transportation back to the British base.

were within 400 yards; then I gave the signal, and we let them have magazine after magazine. All along the front we could hear the Brens and rifles cracking. The enemy sections stopped, wavered, broke into a double and pushed on, stopped again, and finally dived for shelter among some scattered olive trees. They must have suffered terrible casualties."

Panzers ran head-on against the anti-tank guns. They had no possibility of breaking through, and eventually had to turn and scram for cover. By nightfall on the 6th, Rommel had ordered the retreat. The Desert Fox was finished. On 9th March, he left Tunisia for ever – sick, utterly exhausted and, at last, defeated. Von Arnim took over command for the final stages of the North Africa campaign.

Now, with enemy strength further weakened, the Desert Rats could resume their advance. They pushed forward to the German and Italian defensive lines at Mareth, ready for the last great battle. The enemy positions stretched from the sea up into the mountains, and finished at an area of soft sand, which would be very difficult for tanks to move through. Montgomery nevertheless decided to attempt an outflanking movement through this tricky terrain, while other units engaged the enemy in the centre.

On 20th March Montgomery issued orders to the Desert Rats: "The operations now about to begin will mark the close of the campaign in North Africa. Once the battle starts the eyes of the whole world will be on the 8th Army . . . We will not stop, nor let up, till Tunis has been captured, and the enemy has either given up the struggle or has been pushed into the sea . . . Forward to Tunis! *Drive the enemy into the sea!*"

Mountain victory

The battle of Mareth opened on 20th March with a hard blow delivered by British forces on the right of the line. At the same time, a strong outflanking movement began on the left, spearheaded by New Zealand troops, who had been instructed "to go like hell."

For the next week, the battle in the centre of the position continued at full force, while the troops in the outflanking movement worked their way towards the vital Tebega gap in the mountains. Montgomery sent in further units to strengthen this sweeping movement. "The going is tricky," wrote one soldier. "All afternoon we plough on, rolling, heaving and bouncing in soft sand." Vehicles constantly got stuck in the dust, and had to be dug out. Many were abandoned but, by 26th March, the Desert Rats were ready for the stab at Tebega.

Below American soldiers, in their Willy's Jeep, hurtle across the desert towards Bizerte and Tunis, hoping to cut off the German retreat to the sea (1943).

"Punctually at 3.30 p.m. the fighter-bombers appeared," reported an eye-witness, "squadron after squadron; all along the line of the forward infantry little columns of orange smoke rose up, indicating their positions . . . The bombers made no mistakes and nothing was dropped on us, but for half-an-hour they turned the enemy position into a pandemonium."

Then the Desert Rat tanks arrived to lead the infantry into the attack. "Under cover of the noise and smoke of this bombardment, in clouds of dust, Sherman tanks . . . rumbled up . . . They were moving into position when the guns opened, firing for twenty-three minutes on the enemy positions. At 4.15 p.m., the tanks moved majestically forward, followed closely by our infantry carriers. The infantry climbed out of their pits – where previously there had been nothing visible, there were now hundreds of men, who shook out into long lines and followed on 500 yards behind the tanks . . . The assault was on."

And the assault proved successful. Threatened by this punching attack from the side and rear, the German and Italian units retreated again, back into Tunisia – and into the trap set by the twin advances of the 8th Army and Eisenhower's "Torch" troops. The Desert Rats hurtled onwards towards the coast, aiming for Sfax and Sousse. The British 1st Army and the U.S. II Corps pushed forward in the north towards Bizerte and Tunis.

All these allied fingers were now reaching through the mountains to grab at the retreating enemy. And soon the Germans and Italians were able to retreat no further – behind them lay the sea.

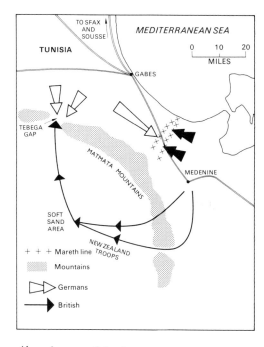

Above A map of the last great battle of the desert war, as New Zealand troops crossed a treacherous area of soft sand to outflank the German forces at Mareth (March, 1943).

Fall of German strongholds

The Desert Rats now moved into increasingly unfamiliar country. Instead of empty wastelands, they fought in green wooded valleys, and scaled range after range of mountains. Some of these peaks were strongly defended by the retreating Germans, and the attempts to wrench the enemy from deep-dug defences cost many lives. One experienced soldier described the return of troops sent to attack such a mountain fortress: "Men . . . have begun drifting back in small groups, most of them badly shaken. They talk of crawling up sheer precipices to find every level expanse swept by machine-gun fire; of wounded rolling all the way down to the bottom; of tripwires, mines and booby-traps on handgrip ledges . . . and of walls and caves and all sorts of cunning defensive devices on the summit, piled round with the dead of previous assaults."

Fighting remained grim, and was often hand-to-hand. The Gurkha troops in the 8th Army, who came from the far-away mountains of Nepal, were particularly expert at close-quarter killing, and delighted in using their grisly short swords or *kukris*. "I crept up," wrote a Gurkha officer, "and found myself looking into the face of a German . . . He was fumbling with his weapon so I cut off his head with my *kukri*. Another appeared from a slit trench and I cut him down too. I was able to do the same to two others, but one made a great deal of noise, which raised the alarm . . . I was now involved in a struggle with a number of Germans, and eventually, after my hands had become cut and slippery with blood, they managed to wrest my *kukri* from me . . . They then beat me to the ground where I lay

86

pretending to be dead."

One by one, the German strongholds fell. Desert Rats entered Sfax on 10th April. Fejna was captured by American troops on 1st May, and Mateur on 3rd May. The ring around Tunis grew tight. On 7th May, the American 34th Division entered Bizerte. And, the same day, men of the 7th Armoured Division, the original Desert Rats, captured Tunis.

At 2.15 p.m., on 13th May, 1943, General Alexander sent a triumphant signal to Winston Churchill in London: "Sir. It is my duty to report that the Tunisian campaign is over. All enemy resistance has ceased. We are masters of the North African shores."

Opposite A map showing how all the fingers of the Allied attack came together to cut off the German retreat.
Below French troops examine the abundant booty which fell into their hands after Rommel's retreat.

Triumph

The last German units had been unable to escape by sea. Nearly 250,000 were herded into captivity, and the victorious Desert Rats watched them as they filed by: "This morning, it's all over . . . We leave the hills and form up in a grove of cactus by the roadside. Along the road northwards, in bright sunshine, passes a never-ending procession of German vehicles – lorries, trucks, ambulances, half-trucks, Volkswagens, motor cycles, Mercedes-Benz staff-cars . . .

"So this is the last of the *Afrika Korps*! The people we've been chasing and been chased by for the last three years, backwards and forwards, over the whole length of North Africa. All the other old adversaries have laid down their arms . . . The Jerries don't look very discouraged, no doubt because they're still intact, and the war's over for them, anyway."

The soldier added: "Tonight the sky is rough with straggling clouds. Tunis and the Carthaginian headland are distinct and dark across the bay . . . the sea has a most extraordinary hue – a pale, malevolent, luminous green. This scene sums up our feelings of anti-climax at the end of the campaign, and of uncertainty about our next move."

Rommel himself had escaped to fight another day, but did not survive the war. The following year, in 1944, he was severely injured during an R.A.F. attack in northern France. Soon afterwards he was accused by Hitler of plotting against him, and was ordered to take his own life.

About 620,000 enemy troops had been killed or captured during the North Africa campaign. British losses totalled 220,000. Most of them belonged to the gallant 8th Army. Many graves marked the path of painful progress across the desert and into the

Below The war cemetery at Alamein, a stark memorial to the Desert Rats who lost their lives in the great conflict.

mountains of Tunisia. A Desert Rat officer wrote: "I thought of those of our people who had died in battle, in a great battle, to their unending, undying honour. For most of them there is a grave in the sand, perhaps a few rocks piled over them, their names in hurried pencil-scrawl upon a cross made of petrol cases.

"For some there is no cross: only a mound of sand that the wind will soon soften and gently erase." But their names live on – the Desert Rats.

Table of dates

1939

1st September	Germany invades Poland.
3rd September	Britain declares war on Germany.

1940

24th May	British troops evacuated from Dunkirk.
10th June	Italy declares war on Britain.
11th June	Directed by Wavell, the Hussars attack the Italians in the North African desert.
7th December	O'Connor's Desert Force overwhelms the Italians at Sidi Barrani.

1941

5th January	Bardia is captured from the Italians.
11th January	Hitler orders that the *Afrika Korps* should be sent to North Africa.
22nd January	Tobruk is captured by the Desert Rats.
5th February	Defeat of the Italians at Beda Fomm. Whole Italian army surrenders.
12th February	Rommel arrives in North Africa to command the *Afrika Korps*.
24th March	Unexpected German advance at El Agheila.
31st March	Rommel's main offensive opens.
6th April	German invasion of Greece. British strength in North Africa is reduced.
10th April	Tobruk is reinforced by Australians.
12th April	Rommel launches repeated attacks against Tobruk, but they fail.
14th June	Wavell begins "Battleaxe" offensive for relief of Tobruk.
17th June	"Battleaxe" fails.
1st July	Auchinleck becomes Middle East Commander.
18th November	Auchinleck starts "Crusader" offensive.
1st December	Rommel pulls back from Sidi-Rezegh.

1942

21st January	Rommel attacks; Desert Rats retreat to Gazala.
27th May	Battle of Gazala begins.
11th June	British retreat from Gazala.
21st June	Tobruk falls to the Germans. Desert Rats retreat to Alamein.
August	Alexander and Montgomery arrive in Egypt.
31st August	Rommel attacks at Alam Halfa without success.
3rd September	Rommel forced to retire from Alam Halfa.
23rd October	Battle of Alamein begins.
2nd November	"Supercharge" breakthrough at Alamein.
8th November	"Torch" landings in French North Africa.
12th November	Rommel retreats into Libya.
17th December	El Agheila is recaptured by the Desert Rats.

1943

23rd January	Allied troops enter Tripoli.
14th February	Rommel counter-attacks at Kasserine.
23rd February	Rommel is again forced to retreat.
6th March	Rommel attacks at Medenine, but fails.
9th March	Rommel leaves North Africa.
20th March	Battle of Mareth begins.
26th March	Final offensive at Mareth. Retreat of Italian and German forces.
10th April	Sfax is captured.
1st May	Fejna is captured.
7th May	Allied troops enter Bizerte and Tunis.
13th May	Surrender of last German units left in North Africa.

Glossary

AFRIKA KORPS The German army serving in North Africa.

BREN-GUN A lightweight machine-gun.

CATERPILLAR TRACK An articulated steel band which passes round the wheels of a tank, for example, or a tractor, to enable it to travel over uneven ground.

DYSENTERY A serious stomach upset, which is accompanied by violent cramps and diarrhoea.

FLANK The right or left-hand side of an army or body of troops. Hence "to outflank" means to sweep round the side of the enemy.

GURKHAS Native troops from Nepal who served with the British army.

INTER-COM An abbreviation of "intercommunications," which is used to describe a short-range radio.

JERBOA A desert rat.

KUKRI A short, sharp sword used by the Gurkhas in hand-to-hand fighting.

MINEFIELD An area which has been planted with explosive mines so that the enemy cannot cross it.

MORTAR A small cannon, which fires shells at high angles over hills and other obstacles, to strike at the troops sheltering on the other side.

PANZER A German tank or armoured car.

TRACER A bullet, the heat of which makes its track visible through the air.

TRENCH A deep ditch used by soldiers for cover, and sometimes for living quarters.

U-BOAT A German submarine.

WADI A watercourse which is dry except in the rainy season.

Slang words used by the Desert Rats

BIVVY A bivouac, or temporary camp.

BOCHE A contemptuous word used to describe the Germans.

BUCKSHEE Free.

BUDDLY To swop.

CHAR Tea.

CHINA Friend.

DUFF No good.

IMBASHA Corporal.

JERRY German.

KOOLOO The whole lot, the entire amount.

PEACHY Soon.

SCOFF Food. To eat.

SHUFTY Take a look.

TARO Just a minute.

ZIFT Bad.

Further Reading

Anon. *They Sought Out Rommel* (H.M.S.O., 1942) – a diary of the Libyan campaign, 16th November to 31st December, 1941, written by one of the infantrymen who took part, and published in a wartime series called "The Army at War."

Carver, Michael, *Tobruk* (Batsford, 1964) – deals mainly with the fighting around Tobruk between November 1941 and June 1942, and contains many excellent eye-witness accounts.

Churchill, Winston, *The Second World War,* Volumes II, III and IV (Cassell, 1950–1951) – Churchill's war history, written in his most descriptive style.

Connell, John, *Wavell: Soldier and Scholar* (Collins, 1966) – a sympathetic and moving biography of the general whom Rommel considered to be his most skilled opponent.

Crimp, R. L., *The Diary of a Desert Rat* (Leo Cooper, 1971) – evocative and personal descriptions of war at the "sharp end."

Montgomery, Viscount, *Memoirs* (Collins, 1958) – "Monty's" version of events, which reflect his individual and outspoken manner.

Strawson, John, *The Battle for North Africa* (Batsford, 1969) – comprehensive history of the desert campaigns, including many eye-witness accounts.

Young, Desmond, *Rommel* (Collins, 1950) – the best biography of the Desert Fox, with a foreword by Auchinleck.

Index

Picture Credits

The Publishers wish to thank the following for their kind permission to reproduce copyright illustrations on the pages mentioned: the Trustees of the Imperial War Museum, *jacket* (front and flaps); the Conway Picture Library, *jacket* (back), 17, 30 (top), 44, 88–89; Keystone Press Agency, *frontispiece*, 9, 10, 12, 13, 14, 21, 29, 42, 47, 51, 56, 57, 58, 59, 69, 71, 73 (top), 75 (top), 77, 81, 82, 84, 87; Popperfoto, 11, 16, 27, 28, 36–37, 52, 64, 65, 83; Fox Photos, 22, 32, 67; the Radio Times Hulton Picture Library, 33, 62.
The maps and diagrams were done by Clive Gordon Associates.